SCHOLASTIC discover more™

explorers

By Penelope Arlon
and Tory Gordon-Harris

Free digital book

Read exciting and up-to-date stories about the people who are exploring Earth and space right now in your free digital book.

21st-century explorers

A digital companion to Explorers

Download your all-new digital book,

21st-Century Explorers

Log on to
www.scholastic.com/discovermore

Enter this special code:
RCFFM7P29TXF

2

Skiing to the poles

Many people take trips after they retire . . . but not many decide to trek to both poles! Barbara Hillary made her first polar expedition in 2007. She was 75! She hadn't even skied before deciding to go on her adventure. For six months, Hillary trained hard. She learned to ski. She would need to pull a heavy sled full of supplies in the Arctic, so she practiced by dragging tyres up her street in Queens, New York! She reached the North Pole in April 2007.

But Hillary didn't stop there. Four years later, she made it to the South Pole. She was 79!

Adventurer in brief	
Nationality	American
Birthday	12 June, 1931
North Pole	23 April, 2007
South Pole	31 January, 2011

Barbara Hillary returns home safely after her adventure in Antarctica in 2011!

The South Pole
A sign and the American flag tell trekkers that they have reached the South Pole. They are repositioned every New Year's Day – because the ice moves about 10 metres (33 feet) every year.

" I want America to see me not as a little old lady – I am an older adventurer. "
—Barbara Hillary

✛ **Her journey**

❓ **Test yourself**

Read incredible true stories, like how one extraordinary woman started exploring when she was over 60 years old!

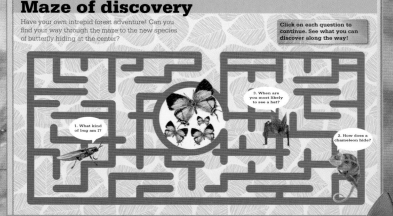

Maze of discovery

Have your own intrepid forest adventure! Can you find your way through the maze to the new species of butterfly hiding at the center?

Click on each question to continue. See what you can discover along the way!

1. What kind of bug am I?

2. How does a chameleon hide?

3. When are you most likely to see a bat?

There are fun activities and quizzes for you to enjoy.

Mount Mabu marvels

When Dr. Julian Bayliss and his team discovered a lost forest in Mozambique, they also found new animals. The Mount Mabu discoveries included snakes, butterflies, bats, and a tiny chameleon.

Dr. Julian Bayliss used a huge net to catch butterflies and flying insects. The creatures were not harmed.

① Bayliss's chameleon
Dr. Bayliss was the first person to discover this species (or kind) of chameleon. So it was named after him!

Name	*Nadzikambia baylissi*
Length	13.2–15.9 cm (5.2–6.3 ins)

② Thyolo alethe
This small bird is one of 126 bird species the team saw at Mount Mabu. It is very rare—it lives only in mountain forests in the area.

Name	*Alethe choloensis*
Length	about 17–19 cm (6.7–7.5 ins)

③ Pygmy chameleon
Another new chameleon Dr. Bayliss found is this tiny pygmy chameleon. It is about the size of a thumb and has a very short tail!

Name	*Rhampholeon sp.*
Length	up to 10 cm (4 ins)

④ African butterfly
The Mount Mabu forest is full of butterflies. The team spotted 203 different kinds, including 4 new species. This is one of them.

Name	*Epamera sp.*
Length	information not yet available

⑤ Mount Mabu forest viper
In 2005, a young viper was found on the forest floor. This tiny venomous snake had never before been seen anywhere in the world.

Name	*Atheris mabuensis*
Length	up to 38.4 cm (15.1 ins)

It's simple to get your digital book. Go to the website (see left), enter the code, and download the book. Make sure you open it using Adobe Reader.

Consultant:
Phyllis C. Hunter

Copyright © 2015 by Scholastic Inc.

All rights reserved. Published by Scholastic Inc.,
Publishers since 1920. SCHOLASTIC, SCHOLASTIC DISCOVER MORE™,
and associated logos are trademarks and/or registered
trademarks of Scholastic Inc.

No part of this publication may be reproduced, stored
in a retrieval system, or transmitted in any form or by any
means, electronic, mechanical, photocopying, recording, or
otherwise, without the written permission of the publisher.
For information regarding permission, write to
Scholastic Inc., Attention: Permissions Department,
557 Broadway, New York, NY 10012.

Distributed in the UK by
Scholastic UK Ltd
Westfield Road, Southam
Warwickshire, England CV47 0RA

Library of Congress Cataloging-in-Publication
Data Available

ISBN 978 1407 14899 1

10 9 8 7 6 5 4 3 2 1   15 16 17 18 19

Printed in Singapore   46
First published 2015

Scholastic is constantly working to lessen the
environmental impact of our manufacturing
processes. To view our industry-leading
paper procurement policy, visit
www.scholastic.com/paperpolicy.

Contents

Into the unknown

Voyages of discovery

Into the **Unkown**

Whether crossing polar ice, climbing the tallest mountains, or sailing on voyages of discovery, people have always been curious about the lands beyond their homes. For thousands of years, explorers have been yearning to reach new places. They are brave, determined, and often willing to take dangerous risks!

Why explore?

All explorers want to venture into the unknown, and they push themselves to the limit to do it. There are many reasons why they get up and go.

New land

Many thousands of years ago, Native Americans made an amazing journey from Asia to settle in what is now the United States.

Wealth

Some explorers have wanted to plunder new lands for their riches. Hernán Cortés (left) conquered Mexico in the 1500s, robbing the people there.

Knowledge

In the 1800s, Mary Kingsley risked her life travelling African rivers. She learned about local people, plants, and animals.

Distant space

We've explored our planet for thousands of years. Now it's time to explore the universe. Next stop, Mars!

Education and adventure

Today, explorers such as Ed Stafford film and write about their adventures as they travel. Stafford walked the whole length of the River Amazon.

Dark waters

There are vast areas of our planet still to be explored – the oceans! Here, scientist and diver Dr Sylvia Earle waves from an underwater laboratory.

Off we go!

The first explorers walked, rowed boats, or rode animals. Then people invented faster and safer ways to travel. Ships conquered the oceans, and engines now whizz us around. And we can rocket off our planet!

Early explorers travelled by foot.

People have ridden horses since 4000 BCE.

Indian elephants have been used since 2500 BCE.

Viking longships in 1000 CE had flat bottoms to travel in shallow water.

Native Americans made dugout canoes from hollowed tree trunks.

People have ridden camels since 3000 BCE.

The Inuits of the Arctic have always used dog sleds.

Around 2500 BCE, ancient Egyptians built boats with pegs instead of nails.

Some ancient vehicles, such as

66 It's like . . . there's a foot in the small of your back pushing you into space, accelerating wildly straight up, shouldering your way through the air. 99

—Chris Hadfield, NASA astronaut, talking about space shuttle lift-off

Exploring space

In 2001, Chris Hadfield flew over 320 km (200 miles) to the International Space Station.

Explorers travelling to the North and South Poles always use skis.

Galleons sailed across oceans in the 16th century.

20th-century space suit

Soyuz rocket

This yacht sailed around the world in 2012.

21st-century Space Launch System (SLS), a heavy-lift launch vehicle

This Sno-Cat crossed Antarctica in 1957–1958.

Trieste, a deep-diving research vehicle (1960)

Shinkai 6500 submersible (1990)

Where am I?

Imagine a world with no maps or GPS! Early explorers had to venture into the unknown with very little to help them find their way.

Early maps

Around 150 CE, the Greek scholar Ptolemy described how to draw maps. Over 1,000 years later, explorers in the 1400s used his instructions.

Stick chart

Ancient islanders in the Pacific Ocean made stick charts. Shells represented islands, and sticks showed wave patterns. These maps were used until the 20th century!

a map from the 1800s ....

Look closely at this map, which Columbus may have used on his early voyages. What's missing?

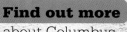

Find out more about Columbus on page 32.

Navigation tools

Explorers need to know exactly where they are and which direction they are going in. Many tools have been invented to help them navigate.

Chip log

Early sailors threw a log tied to a knotted rope off the back of a ship. They could work out speed and distance by counting the knots as the rope unwound.

Compass

Compasses have been in use since as early as 221 BCE.

Sextant

This tool, invented in 1757 and still used today, uses the positions of the Sun and stars to calculate a ship's location.

Mount Mabu

Mount Mabu,
Mozambique

Satellite pictures allow us to zoom in on remote areas

Unexplored forest

Pictures taken by satellites in space allow us to see every corner of the planet. Even so, people who make maps can miss things! In 2005, Dr Julian Bayliss spotted something unusual on Google Earth – he saw a mountain and a rainforest in Mozambique that had never been shown on a map! In 2008, a team of explorers visited the forest and found a treasure trove of undiscovered plants and animals.

This pygmy chameleon had never been seen by scientists before. It lives only on Mount Mabu.

of the world, such as Mount Mabu.

Hall of fame

It's not easy being an explorer. All these famous and not-so-well-known explorers had great courage.

FEARLESS CAVER
In 1842, American slave Stephen Bishop explored and mapped a huge section of the world's longest cave, Mammoth Cave in Kentucky, USA.

SEASICK EXPLORER
Botanist Joseph Banks recorded plants on James Cook's 1768–1771 voyage to the Pacific. He described getting very seasick – poor Banks!

DEEPEST TWEET
"Just arrived at the ocean's deepest pt. Hitting bottom never felt so good. Can't wait to share what I'm seeing w/ you" – adventurer and film director James Cameron, 2012

INTREPID WOMAN
From 1872 to 1904, Isabella Bird travelled alone to Australia, Asia, Africa, and the Americas. She was planning another trip to China when she died at age 72.

CONFIDENT SAILOR
Joshua Slocum sailed around the world from 1895 to 1898, the first person to do so solo. Amazingly, he didn't know how to swim!

America was named after Amerigo Vespucci, an Italian

WELL-DRESSED CLIMBER
In 1838, Henriette d'Angeville climbed Mont Blanc, the highest peak in the Alps, in a skirt! At the top, she drank a glass of champagne.

FIRST SIGHT
In around 1000 CE, Viking explorer Leif Eriksson was the first European to see and land in North America. He called it Vinland.

GLOBAL CYCLIST
From 1894 to 1895, Annie Londonderry bicycled around the world, becoming the first woman to do so. She carried only a change of clothes and a revolver!

FIRST SPACE SELFIE
Neil Armstrong stood on the Moon in 1969. He took this picture of his own image reflected in Buzz Aldrin's helmet!

WORLDLY GOAT
James Cook took a goat on one of his world voyages for its milk. It had already travelled around the world before!

explorer who sailed there from Spain in 1497.

Bold journeys

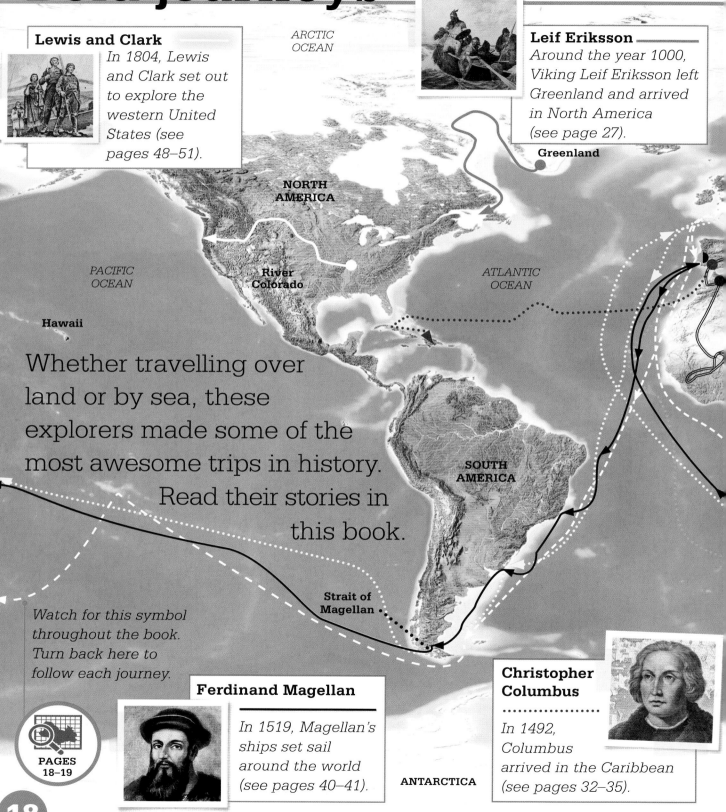

Lewis and Clark
In 1804, Lewis and Clark set out to explore the western United States (see pages 48–51).

ARCTIC OCEAN

Leif Eriksson
Around the year 1000, Viking Leif Eriksson left Greenland and arrived in North America (see page 27).

Greenland

NORTH AMERICA

PACIFIC OCEAN

River Colorado

ATLANTIC OCEAN

Hawaii

Whether travelling over land or by sea, these explorers made some of the most awesome trips in history. Read their stories in this book.

SOUTH AMERICA

Strait of Magellan

Watch for this symbol throughout the book. Turn back here to follow each journey.

PAGES 18–19

Ferdinand Magellan
In 1519, Magellan's ships set sail around the world (see pages 40–41).

ANTARCTICA

Christopher Columbus
In 1492, Columbus arrived in the Caribbean (see pages 32–35).

Check out Ibn Battuta's long route. He had only camels

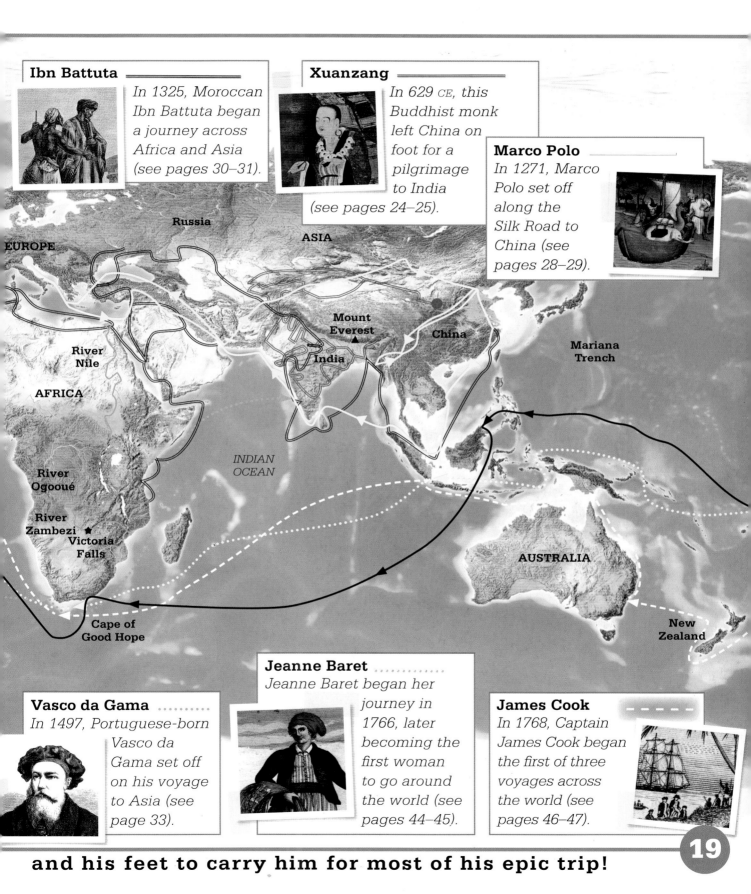

Ibn Battuta

In 1325, Moroccan Ibn Battuta began a journey across Africa and Asia (see pages 30–31).

Xuanzang

In 629 CE, this Buddhist monk left China on foot for a pilgrimage to India (see pages 24–25).

Marco Polo

In 1271, Marco Polo set off along the Silk Road to China (see pages 28–29).

Russia

ASIA

EUROPE

Mount Everest ▲

China

Mariana Trench

River Nile

India

AFRICA

INDIAN OCEAN

River Ogooué

River Zambezi ★ Victoria Falls

AUSTRALIA

New Zealand

Cape of Good Hope

Vasco da Gama

In 1497, Portuguese-born Vasco da Gama set off on his voyage to Asia (see page 33).

Jeanne Baret

Jeanne Baret began her journey in 1766, later becoming the first woman to go around the world (see pages 44–45).

James Cook

In 1768, Captain James Cook began the first of three voyages across the world (see pages 46–47).

and his feet to carry him for most of his epic trip!

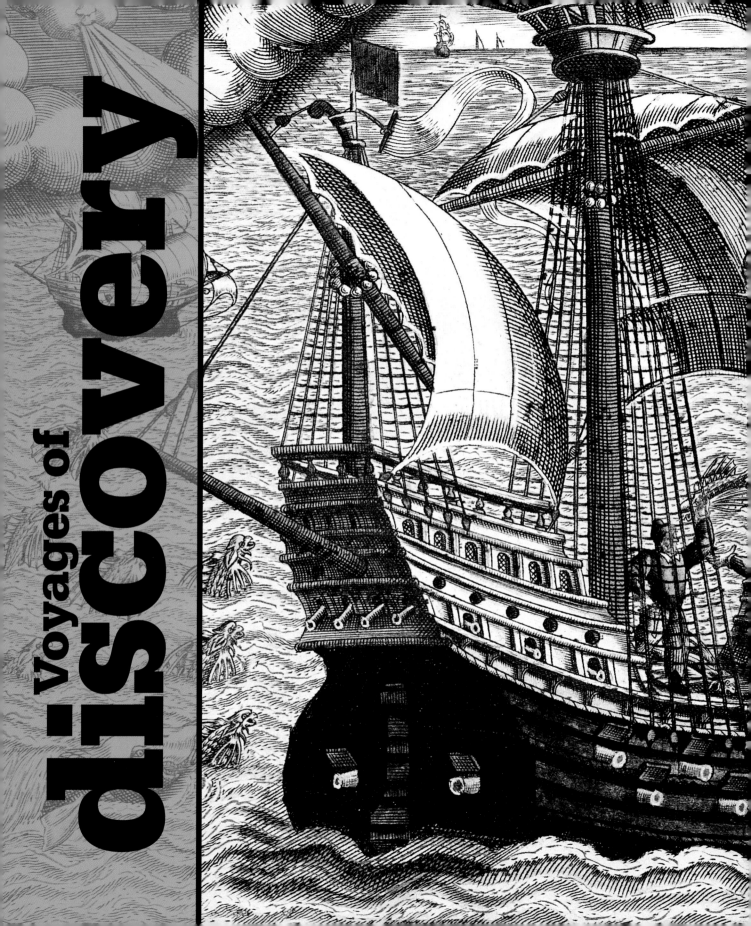

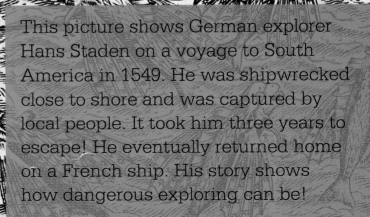

This picture shows German explorer Hans Staden on a voyage to South America in 1549. He was shipwrecked close to shore and was captured by local people. It took him three years to escape! He eventually returned home on a French ship. His story shows how dangerous exploring can be!

Famous ancient explorers

Not much is known about ancient explorers. Stories of their exploits had to be carved in stone, recorded on ancient manuscripts, or passed down as spoken tales.

c.1460 BCE

Stone carvings tell how the Egyptian queen Hatshepsut sent ships to the land of Punt to bring back riches. Today, nobody is quite sure exactly where Punt was!

c.1000 BCE

Testing DNA (a substance found in all living things) has shown that people from Taiwan settled on the Polynesian islands in the Pacific Ocean.

c.500 BCE

A Greek manuscript describes how Hanno the Navigator, from northern Africa, travelled by boat down the African coast.

Tales of ancient adventures are often full of strange

c.330 BCE

An ancient Greek named Pytheas sailed north. He described vast icebergs and giant fish as big as boats. He must have sailed as far north as the Arctic Circle!

c.220 BCE

Tales of Chinese explorer Xu Fu were passed down as spoken stories. About 1,000 years later, his story was finally written down. The Chinese emperor sent him to find magic plants. He made it to Japan.

c.520 CE

The voyage of Saint Brendan of Clonfert is legendary in Ireland. He sailed into the Atlantic Ocean, looking for the Garden of Eden.

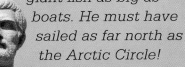

lands and dangerous sea monsters.

The adventures of . . .

XUANZANG

If you need to check a fact, you can look it up online or in a library. You couldn't do that in 629 CE! In that year, a Chinese Buddhist monk named Xuanzang (shoo-wen-zahng) thought the Buddhist writings he read had some mistakes. So he decided to travel to India, where Buddhism came from. He was on the road for 16 years!

Xuanzang had some incredible adventures. He had to sneak out of China, dodging sentries with bows and arrows. He got lost and almost died in the dangerous Gobi desert.

Buddha

Xuanzang travelled along a long stretch of the Silk Road.

On his journey, Xuanzang met many kings and built up a following of people and horses. Unfortunately, half of Xuanzang's crew died in the freezing Tian Shan mountain range.

Xuanzang finally reached India and spent many years studying Buddhism there. He returned to China with many followers — and a lot of luggage!

Tian Shan mountains

Gobi desert

China

India

Xuanzang arrived back in China with more than 600 books, gold statues, relics, lots of information, and some excellent stories. His tales were so interesting that the Chinese emperor made him write them all down, which is why we know about his adventures today.

Turn to page 28 to find out more about this route.

Vikings!

Starting around 800 CE, fierce Vikings – from Norway, Sweden, and Denmark – sailed around the North Atlantic in longships. They looked for lands and treasures to plunder.

Longships
These simple boats were fast and light. The seas were often freezing – those Vikings were tough!

1 The keel
A longship's keel (bottom) was carved, then held in place with wooden blocks.

2 The sides
Overlapping planks were nailed together to make the sides of the boat.

3 The prow
A dragon's head was carved on the prow (front) of the boat. It was sometimes decorated with gold and silver to glint in the sunlight.

Longships could sail up the shallowest rivers. They

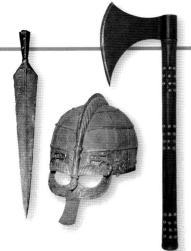

TRUE STORY: Viking mother

Name: Gudrid Thorbjarnardottir
Nationality: Viking
Where: North America
When: c.1010 CE

This intrepid woman travelled on a longship from Greenland to North America. She gave birth to possibly the first European baby born in America. Later in life, she may have travelled to Italy to meet the Pope!

Follow my journey
PAGE 18

Viking raiders

793
Vikings attacked a monastery on the English island of Lindisfarne.

982
Viking leader Erik the Red, banished from Iceland, explored and settled in Greenland.

1000
Erik the Red's son, Leif Eriksson, was the first European to reach and settle in America. He called it Vinland.

1010
Viking Gudrid Thorbjarnardottir gave birth to a son in Vinland.

1066
King Harold of England, from a Danish family, was defeated by William the Conqueror at the Battle of Hastings.

4 **The mast**
The mast was raised. Stones were added to keep the ship stable.

5 **A single square**
Finally, the sail was raised. Oarsmen had to bring their own trunks to sit on!

could also be carried across land by hand!

Marco Polo

In 1271, 17-year-old Marco Polo left Venice for a journey to the East. He travelled on the Silk Road, a trade route between Europe and China. It was more than 6,400 km (4,000 miles) – that's a long way by foot or camel!

Silk Road trade

Europeans wanted silks and spices from China. The Chinese wanted goods such as silver and horses from many of the countries along the Silk Road.

The spice star anise is grown in China. It tastes like liquorice!

WEST

EAST

TRUE STORY: The birth of the Silk Road

Name: Zhang Qian
Nationality: Chinese
Where: The Silk Road
When: 138 BCE
How: Foot, horse, or camel

In about 138 BCE, the emperor of China sent Zhang Qian (pronounced "jang chyen") to explore the world to the west. Zhang Qian left China with camels and 100 soldiers. His route set the trail for the Silk Road.

The bubonic plague, a sickness that killed millions of people, spread along the Silk Road in 1346. It was carried by rats.

Marco Polo told wild

Treacherous path

The Silk Road wasn't a straight, paved, easy road. Traders had to cross scorching deserts, snowy mountains, and many kingdoms. Bloodthirsty bandits lined the route, ready to steal their possessions.

The Silk Road (shown in red) stretched from Europe to China. Polo's route is shown in yellow.

Venice · Iran · Mongolia · Israel · China

Marco Polo's journey, 1271–1295

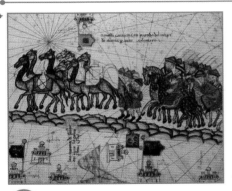

1 Departure

Polo was only 17 when he left Venice (in today's Italy). He sailed to Israel, then journeyed on by camel to Iran.

2 Eastern arrival

After about four years of travelling, he was welcomed at the court of the great Mongolian ruler Kublai Khan.

3 Return home

Polo journeyed nearly 24,000 km (15,000 miles) in 24 years. He headed home on a Chinese ship called a junk.

stories about monstrous birds and people with tails!

The travels of Ibn Battuta

In 1325, Ibn Battuta, a Moroccan Muslim, decided to see as much of the world as he could. In 30 years, he travelled about 121,000 km (75,000 miles) – that's the same as three times around the globe!

Well traveled
Ibn Battuta first headed for the holy city of Mecca (in modern-day Saudi Arabia).

Ibn Battuta almost died of thirst in the desert. He described how the sand stung his eyes.

Follow my journey
PAGES 18–19

Ibn Battuta vowed "never to travel any road a second

The hajj

Many Muslims, like Ibn Battuta, feel that they must visit Mecca at least once in their lifetime. This pilgrimage is known as the hajj.

Ibn Battuta's highlights

Egypt
On the way to Mecca, Ibn Battuta passed through Cairo, Egypt. He described its "beauty and splendour."

dhow

East Africa
After his second hajj, he sailed the Red Sea. He called Zeila, Somalia, the "most stinking town in the world"!

The Maldives
He spent nine months in the Maldives, in the Indian Ocean. He became a judge and married into the royal family.

China
The sultan of India sent Ibn Battuta to China as an ambassador. He wrote about China's beautiful silks and the Great Wall.

Timbuktu
After a short visit home, Ibn Battuta crossed the Sahara to reach the great city of Timbuktu (in today's Mali)!

time". As far as we know, he didn't!

Race to the Far East!

By the late 1400s, the land route from Europe to Asia, the Silk Road, had become very difficult. The powerful nations of Spain and Portugal rushed to find ways to reach Asia by sea.

CHRISTOPHER COLUMBUS

SPONSORED BY
Spain

FLEET
3 ships

Columbus sailed on *Santa María*.

DEPARTED
Spain, August 1492

ARRIVED
Caribbean islands, October 1492

SUCCESS STORY
Columbus was looking for a route to Asia. Instead, he reached the Americas. For the rest of his life he thought they were part of Asia!

NORTH AMERICA

The Caribbean

Portugal

EUROPE

Spain

AFRICA

SOUTH AMERICA

East or west?
Christopher Columbus headed west for Asia. He didn't realize that there was a huge landmass, the Americas, in the way! Da Gama sailed south and east, around Africa.

The Americas were rich with gold.

Spice obsession

European explorers risked their lives to reach Asia to get spices such as pepper and nutmeg. Europe's food must have been very dull!

The Ottoman Empire in Turkey tried to block off the Silk Road to stop trade between Europe and Asia.

The "Spice Islands"

ASIA
India

AUSTRALIA

Who won?

Both did! Da Gama sailed to India, succeeding in his mission to find a new route to Asia. Columbus didn't reach Asia – but he did open up the New World to exploration!

VASCO DA GAMA

SPONSORED BY
Portugal

FLEET
4 ships

Da Gama sailed on *São Gabriel*.

DEPARTED
Portugal, July 1497

ARRIVED
India, May 1498

SUCCESS STORY
Da Gama was the first person to discover a trade route to Asia by sea. This expanded Portugal's empire into Asia.

Exploring the Americas

It didn't take Europeans long to realize that Columbus had found something even more valuable than the Spice Islands. They rushed to explore and claim North and South America.

Land ahoy!

Columbus landed on a Caribbean island in 1492. He named it San Salvador. Over four voyages, he claimed many islands and parts of Central America for Spain.

Columbus found the local Taino people of San Salvador friendly.

TRUE STORY: Columbus' rescuer

Name: Guacanagarix
Job: Taino chief
Where: Hispaniola (a Caribbean island)
When: 1492

Columbus' ship Santa María was wrecked on Hispaniola. Guacanagarix helped Columbus, allowing his crew to shelter there. Without Guacanagarix, Columbus might not have survived!

Colonists

European colonists settled on the Native Americans' land. They brought diseases that wiped out whole tribes, such as the Tainos, forever.

The Pilgrims

In 1620, a group of religious pilgrims from Europe sailed to North America. They landed there and made it their new home. They were some of the first settlers in what would be a brand-new country, the United States.

> **Find out more**
> about American explorers on pages 48–51.

1492

Columbus landed on the Caribbean island of San Salvador.

1497

John Cabot landed in Newfoundland, Canada. He claimed it for England.

1607

The first permanent English colony in North America was Jamestown, named after King James.

1608

Samuel de Champlain set up a permanent French colony in Canada. He explored the Great Lakes.

1609

Henry Hudson sailed up the River Hudson and claimed it for the Netherlands.

The conquistadors

After Columbus, Spanish explorers rushed to the Americas – particularly when gold was discovered!

Hernán Cortés

Francisco Pizarro

Cortés and Pizarro

The Spanish conquerors were known as conquistadors. Two of them, Cortés and Pizarro, stormed through the Americas, destroying whole cultures. They seized lands and stole treasures.

The end of the Incas

Atahuallpa, the emperor of the great Inca civilization in South America, welcomed Pizarro. In return, the conquistador killed Atahuallpa and took his city.

Machu Picchu was a magnificent Inca city in Peru. It was abandoned after the Spanish conquest.

Some think that the gold taken back to Spain would be

EYEWITNESS Gold quest

> **"We Spaniards know a sickness of the heart that only gold can cure."**
>
> —Hernán Cortés

South American gold

South Americans valued gold as an offering to the gods. It was not used as money.

El Dorado

Rumours spread in Spain that a city of gold, known as El Dorado, existed in South America. Nobody knew where it was, but the conquistadors were desperate to find it.

worth £1.8 trillion today!

Conquistador timeline

1513
Juan Ponce de León, who travelled with Columbus, was the first European to explore Florida.

1521
Hernán Cortés defeated the Aztec people in Mexico.

1532
Francisco Pizarro conquered the Inca civilization in Peru.

1541
Hernando de Soto explored what is now the southeastern United States and crossed the River Mississippi.

1542
Juan Rodríguez Cabrillo led the first exploration up the coast of California.

Hot chocolate!

In 1519, the Aztec emperor Montezuma II met the conquistador Cortés. Montezuma served frothy liquid chocolate to Cortés and his men. Cortés couldn't get enough! When Cortés overthrew the emperor, he took cacao beans back to Spain. The royal family loved chocolate so much, they kept its recipe a secret for 100 years!

Montezuma was a very successful and powerful ruler until he was defeated by Cortés.

The Aztecs drank chocolate flavoured with chillies.

cacao beans

The Spanish sweetened it.

Around the world

In 1519, Ferdinand Magellan set out with a fleet of ships to sail west past the Americas to Asia. One of his ships then continued past Asia and returned to Europe. It was the first ship to sail around the world!

Under Spanish flag

Magellan was Portuguese. He argued with his king. So Spain supported his big adventure.

Setting sail

Magellan left Spain in 1519 with 5 huge galleons and 237 men. He sailed west, like Columbus had, and went around the bottom of South America.

Magellanic penguins were named after the explorer who was the first to see them.

Some people at the time thought that the world was

A tough journey

Mutiny

Near South America, some of the crew, including Juan Sebastián de Elcano, mutinied. They failed.

In a mutiny, crew members try to take control of a ship from the captain.

Starvation

In the Pacific, the crew ran out of food. They ate maggot-filled biscuits and sawdust. In 1521, they reached the Spice Islands.

Tragedy

A fight broke out on one island, and Magellan was killed. Elcano later took over *Victoria*. In 1522, the ship arrived back in Spain.

TRUE STORY: The final voyage

Name: Juan Sebastián de Elcano
Nationality: Spanish
Where: Around the world
When: 1519–1522

Magellan held Elcano in chains after the mutiny. He later forgave him. When Magellan died, Elcano took over Victoria. Only he and 17 others from the original crew made it home.

SPEED AROUND THE WORLD

Magellan's crew needed almost three years to sail around the world. Check out these speed records:

WIND-POWERED BOAT

In 2012, Loïck Peyron took 45 days, 13 hours, 42 minutes, and 53 seconds to sail around the world.

HOT-AIR BALLOON

In 2002, Steve Fossett took just over 13 days to fly nonstop around the world in a balloon, solo.

BICYCLE

In 2010, Alan Bate cycled around the world in 125 days, 21 hours, and 45 minutes. That included the time he spent crossing oceans on a boat!

flat. This trip proved once and for all that it was round!

A sailor's life

Life was hard for a 16th-century sailor. If he didn't die from exhaustion, drowning, or a pirate attack, a nasty disease called scurvy might have killed him!

There were no toilets. Instead, sailors hung over the deck railing!

The captain slept at the back. The crew slept anywhere!

A crewman steered the ship by moving a long pole attached to the rudder.

This ship, *Golden Hind*, travelled around the world

Hazards

Rats were a huge problem. They ate food and spread diseases. Every ship had a cat to kill rats.

Sailors often had to climb up the rigging to fix the sails. Imagine climbing wet ropes in a storm!

The huge cannons were tied in place with ropes to keep them from shifting and squashing the crew.

Sailors didn't bathe often. Each brought only one set of clothes. Smelly!

Sailors ate meat and cheese. Biscuits might be filled with maggots. Yuck!

smelly socks

Sailors who died at sea were wrapped in old sails. Then they were thrown overboard.

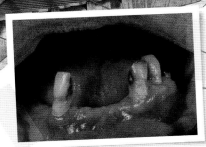

Death by scurvy

Lack of fresh fruit led to the disease scurvy. A sailor's hair and teeth fell out. His body turned black and blue!

Freshwater supplies had to last the entire trip. Water was kept in barrels.

from 1577 to 1580 with Sir Francis Drake as captain.

The adventures of . . .

Follow my journey
PAGES
18–19

JEANNE BARET

Back in 1766, it was unusual (and illegal in some countries) for a woman to board an explorer's ship. But French plant expert Jeanne Baret didn't let that keep her from her studies.

Baret worked as an assistant to botanist Philibert Commerçon, who was invited to join an around-the-world expedition. He and Baret hatched a plan — she joined the party disguised as a boy! She wore bandages around her body to give her a more manly shape. For years, nobody guessed her secret.

Jeanne Baret

When the expedition reached South America, Baret and Commerçon collected many interesting plants. They studied them to use in medicine.

herbal medicines

Baret didn't set out to be the first woman to sail around

bougainvillea, found by Baret and named
after the ship's captain, de Bougainville

Then the expedition arrived at the island of Tahiti, in the Pacific Ocean. A local guest visited the ship and commented on how unusual it was for a woman to be on board. The Tahitian saw right through Baret's disguise, and her cover was blown!

Baret and Commerçon collected about 6,000 plants. About 70 were named after Commerçon. In 2012, one was finally named after Baret.

Solanum baretiae,
named after Jeanne Baret

Captain Louis-Antoine de Bougainville left Baret and Commerçon on the island of Mauritius, in the Indian Ocean. Perhaps he was embarrassed to arrive home with a woman on his ship! After Commerçon's death, Baret returned to France. Upon landing, she became the first woman to have sailed around the globe. What a heroine!

45

the world. She just wanted to explore and discover plants.

Captain Cook

In 1768, 1772, and 1776, Englishman James Cook set sail on three voyages of exploration. He had a top secret mission from the king of England!

HMS *Endeavour*

Cook was born into a poor family. He worked on merchant ships as a young man. In 1768, he was put in charge of a ship named *Endeavour*.

Follow my journey

PAGES 18–19

The secret mission

King George III gave Cook a secret message. It instructed him to search for an enormous continent at the bottom of the world. Cook didn't find it on his first voyage, so he tried again on his second.

Find out more about navigation tools on page 13.

Joseph Banks travelled with Cook. He may have been

The voyages south

The first voyage
Cook sailed to Tahiti, in the Pacific Ocean, where his crew learned how to tattoo! He then claimed eastern Australia for England.

The second voyage
This mission took Cook further south than anyone had ever been before. As he neared Antarctica, he realized it was too cold to land on!

The final voyage
In 1776, Cook – now a captain – left to find a route to the Pacific through the Arctic. He reached Hawaii in 1779. A fight broke out there, and Cook was killed.

Where on Earth . . . ?
Cook was one of the first explorers to use a chronometer. This was an accurate clock that helped sea explorers determine where they were.

the first European to see a kangaroo – which he ate!

Lewis and Clark

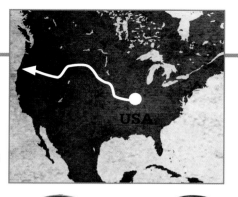

In 1803, US president Thomas Jefferson bought a vast area of land from the French. He needed someone to explore and map this new territory, then continue all the way west to the Pacific Ocean.

Meriwether Lewis

William Clark

American adventure

Jefferson sent his secretary, Meriwether Lewis, who asked his friend William Clark to join him. With about 40 other men, they spent over two years (1804–1806) braving raging rivers, bitterly cold mountains, and ferocious wild animals.

Survival in the wild

Building boats

Where they could, they travelled along rivers. They often had to abandon boats and build new ones.

When food

Lewis and Clark found the Native American people mostly friendly and helpful.

Head flatteners

Along the River Columbia, Lewis and Clark came across the Clatsop people. In his diary, Clark showed how these Native Americans flattened their heads!

Lewis and Clark recorded 300 new species of plants and animals in their diaries.

Gathering food

They had to find food along the way. They carried rifles for hunting animals.

Staying alive!

Wild animals were often a problem. Lewis had to run into a river to escape an angry grizzly!

Carrying supplies

The explorers carried all kinds of supplies: mosquito nets, soup, soap, compasses, and 24 spoons!

The party ate large deer, including elk.

ran out in the mountains, they had to eat their horses.

Sacagawea

Clark wrote that a   woman's

A guiding hand

Lewis and Clark might not have reached the Pacific coast had it not been for a Native American woman named Sacagawea. She joined their group and found them plants that were safe to eat. She also translated for them, helping them buy horses from a local tribe.

presence made their party less of a threat to locals.

River adventures

During the 1800s, sailing down incredible rivers was the ultimate adventure for explorers.

David Livingstone

During the 1850s, Scottish explorer David Livingstone set off on two trips along the River Zambezi in Africa. His goal was to spread Christianity and look for ways to trade.

AFRICA ········ **River Zambezi**

Alexandrine Tinné

In 1861, a female Dutch explorer, Alexandrine Tinné, took her mother and aunt on a river trip. They left Cairo, Egypt, on an expedition to map the course of the River Nile.

AFRICA ········ **River Nile**

John Wesley Powell

Little was known about the Grand Canyon before Powell travelled down the River Colorado. He led the trip with only one arm! He had lost the other in the American Civil War.

Powell

NORTH AMERICA ········ **River Colorado**

River explorers were plagued by mosquitoes, which

Wild animals were a serious danger. Livingstone was mauled by a lion!

Find out more about a modern River Amazon explorer on page 75.

Coast to coast

Livingstone was the first European to cross Africa from east to west. He was also the first European to see the great waterfall on the Zambezi, which he named Victoria Falls.

Ouch!

The women were so badly bitten by mosquitoes that their faces completely swelled up! Tinné didn't find the source of the Nile, but she did reach Sudan.

Raging rapids

In 1869, Powell left with nine men and four boats. For three months, they rode through rapids and flew down waterfalls, and they almost died of starvation.

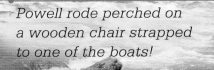

Powell rode perched on a wooden chair strapped to one of the boats!

caused itching and spread the tropical disease malaria.

53

MARY KINGSLEY

In 1893, at the age of 30, Mary Kingsley left England and headed for western Africa alone. She was on a mission to study animals and bring specimens home. On her many African travels, Kingsley got to know local people who taught her how to survive in the wild.

On one trip, down the River Ogooué, Kingsley used her umbrella to prod a large crocodile that was trying to tip her canoe!

In 1899, Kingsley travelled to South Africa to nurse sick

Kingsley wrote fantastic diaries describing her river adventures. She stayed with the Fang people, who were rumoured to be cannibals. But Kingsley was hard to scare! She once fell into an animal trap — a pit with spikes at the bottom. She said that her long, thick skirt saved her from being stabbed by the spikes!

Kingsley returned to England in 1895. Her travels had made her quite famous. She delivered many animal reports to the British Museum and published her travel diaries.

On her adventures, Kingsley once traded 12 of her blouses to get out of a tricky situation with locals.

Price: LIFE

specimen jars

Mary Kingsley wrote that Europeans should respect Africans, instead of stealing their land and treating them unfairly. She believed that all races were equal, and she respected all cultures. Many people at the time disagreed with her.

soldiers. She caught typhoid there, and died in 1900.

Above and **beyond**

By the 20th century, much of the world's land had been explored. Only the most extreme and remote parts of the globe, like the frozen poles and the highest mountains, remained unknown. Explorers also turned to the ocean's mysterious depths – and ultimately left Earth entirely, for space.

The adventures of . . .

MATTHEW HENSON

To survive the cold, polar explorers wore clothes made of seal and polar bear skins.

In the early 1900s, explorers became obsessed with reaching the icy North Pole. American Robert Peary was one of them. On his team was African American Matthew Henson.

Peary met Henson in 1887 and soon sent him to the Arctic Circle to prepare for polar trips. Henson spent years in Greenland, learning the Inuit language and being taught to sled with dogs, hunt, make warm clothes, and build igloos.

Henson was now a valuable member of Peary's team. Peary admired him very much, describing him as his "first man". He never travelled without Henson.

dogs pulling a sled

Henson spent his early life sailing the world. He learned

Robert Peary

Peary and Henson made several attempts to reach the North Pole. On 6 April 1909, Peary, Henson, 4 Inuit men, and 40 dogs finally arrived. They claimed to be the first to set foot on the North Pole.

Igloos are temporary ice shelters.

By the time they arrived, Peary was so exhausted that he was unable to lead the return journey. Henson successfully led the party back to safety. They had covered more than 800 km (500 miles) in 16 days.

Peary's team holds flags at the North Pole.

In 2000, the National Geographic Society finally acknowledged Henson's achievement. He was awarded its highest honour, the Hubbard Medal.

THE HUBBARD MEDAL

NATIONAL GEOGRAPHIC SOCIETY

to read and write on board a ship.

Race across Antarctica

After Peary and Henson reached the North Pole, the next challenge for polar explorers was Antarctica. The South Pole lies in the centre of this brutally cold continent.

Roald Amundsen

In 1910, Norwegian Roald Amundsen and his team travelled to Antarctica. Amundsen wanted to be the first person to reach the South Pole.

19 men

52 dogs

Robert Scott

Robert Scott and his British team also left for Antarctica in 1910. Both teams spent months preparing before starting for the pole in late 1911.

65 men

19 ponies

34 dogs

Scott even took a gramophone!

Find out more about Mount Everest on pages 64–65.

Crossing the continent

Antarctica is incredibly difficult to explore. Vivian Fuchs led the team that first crossed the continent from coast to coast in 1957–1958. They travelled in Sno-Cat tractors.

TRANS-ANTARCTIC EXPEDITION

TUCKER SNO-CAT

It took Fuchs and his team 99 days to cross Antarctica.

Scott's previous trip

Scott had already been to Antarctica. From 1901 to 1904, he led a team on an exploration there. They did lots of scientific research but did not reach the South Pole.

Scott's ship Discovery got stuck in the ice for an entire year!

Triumph!

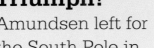

Amundsen left for the South Pole in October 1911, with sleds, dogs, and four men. On 14 December, they reached the pole. All the men returned safely.

the Norwegian flag at the South Pole

Disappointment

Scott and his four men pulled their sleds as they walked. On 17 January 1912, they arrived at the pole but found that they had been beaten. Tragically, they all died on the return trip.

Scott's team at the South Pole

This Sno-Cat carried Fuchs across Antarctica.

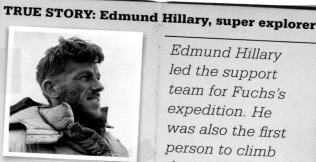

TRUE STORY: Edmund Hillary, super explorer

Name: Edmund Hillary
Nationality: New Zealand
Where: The South Pole
When: 1958
How: Tractor

Edmund Hillary led the support team for Fuchs's expedition. He was also the first person to climb the highest mountain in the world – Mount Everest! What an explorer!

TUCKER SNO-C

61

Scott's hut

The explorers brought a lot of canned and dried food

Life in the hut

Scott and his team brought materials to build huts in Antarctica. They lived and worked in them from 1911 to 1913. This one had a central eating area, and a stove for heat and cooking. There were areas for working and doing research, and these very cramped sleeping bunks!

with them. They also ate their dogs if the dogs died.

Top of the world

Mount Everest is the highest mountain on Earth. Many attempt to scale its terrifying faces. Some die trying to reach the top.

First up!
Edmund Hillary and Tenzing Norgay were the first to make it to the summit. They reached it in 1953.

Danger!
Over 200 people have died trying to climb Everest. It's extremely cold and often windy, and avalanches can happen at any time.

Avalanche

Snow blindness

Frostbite

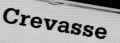

Crevasse

Many climbers have lost their toes to frostbite.

TRUE STORY: Tenzing Norgay

Name: Tenzing Norgay
Nationality: Nepalese
Where: Mount Everest
When: 1953
How: Foot

Without local guides, called Sherpas, no explorer could climb Everest. Sherpas know the dangers and how to avoid them. Tenzing Norgay climbed with Edmund Hillary.

Everest is about 8.8 km

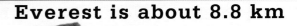

> *I can't understand why men make all this fuss about Everest — it's only a mountain.*
>
> —Junko Tabei

First woman

Japanese climber Junko Tabei was the first woman to climb Everest, in 1975. She was also the first woman to climb the Seven Summits — the highest peak on each continent.

HIGH ACHIEVERS!

YOUNGEST CLIMBER

In 2010, American Jordan Romero climbed to the top of Everest. He was only 13!

HIGHEST FIGHT!

In 1992, two rival Chilean expeditions raced to reach the summit. The winning climbers mocked the runners-up, and some of them pushed others – making it the highest brawl in the world!

FIRST DISABLED PERSON TO THE TOP

In 1998, American Tom Whittaker became the first disabled person to summit. He had an amputated foot.

Frozen boots

One morning, Hillary woke to find that his boots had frozen solid inside the tent. He had to heat them on a camp stove before they could set off again!

(5.5 miles) high. That's the height that jets cruise at!

Under the earth

You might think that most of our planet has been explored by now. But that is far from the truth. Explorers are as busy and excited today as they were thousands of years ago. Next stop, underground!

Er Wang Dong Cave

In 2013, Robbie Shone and his team discovered a gigantic cave in China. It has a room so big, it has its own weather – including clouds and fog!

"It is always very special, knowing that you are the

Amazing caves

Longest cave
The world's longest cave system is Mammoth Cave in Kentucky, with 644 km (400 miles) explored. It was mapped by a slave, Stephen Bishop, in 1842.

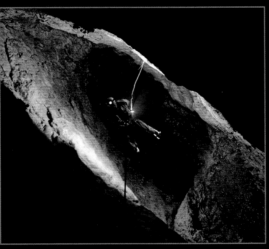

Deepest cave
Gennadiy Samokhin set a record of −2,197 m (−7,208 ft) in Krubera Cave in Georgia. He swam through part of it! Jill Heinerth also swims in caves. She's one of the world's top cave divers.

Icy caves
British caver Robbie Shone has also descended into ice caves in glaciers. These caves change shape as the ice melts and water carves out hollows.

first to step foot into a cave," Robbie Shone says.

Humans in space

Humans have been exploring Earth for thousands of years. But space exploration has been going on for barely 50! A lot has been achieved in that time.

1961
Soviet Yuri Gagarin was the first person to travel into space. He flew all the way around Earth.

1963
Soviet Valentina Tereshkova was the first woman in space. She spent three days there.

1969
American Neil Armstrong was the first human to set foot on our Moon.

2000
American William Shepherd was the first person to live on and command the International Space Station (ISS).

In 1971, Alan Shepard was the first person to hit a golf ball on the Moon. It travelled for kilometres!

1984
American Bruce McCandless was the first astronaut to float in space without a safety line.

Astronauts on the ISS explore how we can

2007

American Sunita Williams ran the first marathon in space. She completed the Boston Marathon on a treadmill in 4 hours, 24 minutes.

The future

MISSION: ASTEROID

NASA and partners are planning a robotic mission to capture an asteroid. Astronauts will then fly to it, conduct space walks on it, and bring back samples.

2013

Canadian Chris Hadfield filmed himself singing David Bowie's "Space Oddity" on the ISS – and got over 20 million hits on YouTube!

WANTED! PERSON TO FLY TO MARS

The race is on to send a person to Mars. NASA hopes to send astronauts by the 2030s. It may take over a year to fly there!

live away from Earth.

Ocean depths

They're freezing and pitch-black, and the pressure could crush you. The seas are the hardest places in the world to explore!

Taking the plunge

The Mariana Trench, in the Pacific, is the deepest part of the ocean. It is more than 2,000 m deeper than Mount Everest is tall. Wow – that's really deep!

" Within a minute or two I'm out of sunlight, and you're in total darkness for most of this dive, so the sub gets very cold, and you have to put on warm clothing. "

—James Cameron, 2012, diving down the Mariana Trench

0 m

1,000

2,000

3,000

4,000

40 m (130 ft)

In 1829, the Deane brothers tested their new diving helmet. They dived to about 40 m (130 ft).

290 m (950 ft)

In 2014, Will Goodman set the record for the deepest scuba dive – 290 m (950 ft)!

Shinkai 6500

3,800 m (12,500 ft)

In 1985, Dr Robert Ballard located Titanic's shipwreck 3,800 m (12,500 ft) deep. An unmanned submersible called Argo took the first images of it.

wreck of **Titanic**

DEEPSEA CHALLENGER

10,908 m (35,787 ft)

In 2012, James Cameron dived to the bottom of the Mariana Trench in Deepsea Challenger. It took just over two and a half hours to get there.

6,500 m (21,300 ft)

In 2013, Dr Ken Takai led an expedition in the Shinkai 6500 submersible to explore the deepest deep-sea vents ever found.

8,200 m (26,900 ft)

In 1872–1876, HMS Challenger dropped ropes and dredges to map the ocean floor and bring up samples. 4,714 new animal species were found.

10,911 m (35,797 ft)

In 1960, Jacques Piccard and Don Walsh dived in the submersible Trieste. They reached the deepest point on Earth – the Mariana Trench.

5,000   6,000   7,000   8,000   9,000   10,000   11,000

Interview with an

Name:
Dr Cindy Lee Van Dover
Profession:
Deep-sea biologist

Q **Where is your favourite area to dive?**

A I love to dive pretty much anywhere, but it is especially exciting to dive somewhere no one has ever been before. There is a lot of opportunity for that in the ocean!

Q **When did you become interested in the ocean?**

A I grew up near the shore in New Jersey, USA. When I was a kid, we would go to the beach. I loved finding and studying shells, mole crabs, horseshoe crabs, and tide pools.

scaly-foot snail

Q **What is the most fascinating thing you have discovered?**

A The shrimp that occur at hot springs, because they have unusual eyes. Instead of normal black, beady shrimp eyes, they have eyes that have disappeared into their bodies. They can't see like we do – instead, they see very dim light.

Q **What is your favourite sea creature?**

A I am very fond of the scaly-foot snail that we discovered near hot springs in the Indian Ocean. It has metal scales on its foot!

ocean explorer

Q You have just returned from a dive in the brand-new *Alvin* submersible. What were you studying?

A Weirdly enough, lakes at the bottom of the ocean! In the Gulf of Mexico, salt on the seafloor dissolves, leaving big holes. The dissolved salt mixes with seawater, making a thick brine that sits in the holes. We are studying the animals that live on the shores of these lakes.

..........*Alvin*

Q What does it feel like to sink deep down in *Alvin*?

A At first the water is sunlit; then it suddenly gets very dark. We sink without lights, so we can see any creatures that create light (called bioluminescence). At the bottom, we turn on the lights and get a great view. The water is so clear.

Q What is the weirdest sea creature you have seen?

A Wow, that's a tough one! I think giant tube worms are weird. They are as tall as I am, with no mouths and no stomachs!

Q If you could be any ocean creature, what would it be?

A While the scaly-foot snail is pretty neat, I think I would like to be a giant squid. I could explore the deepest parts of the ocean.

Q Why is ocean exploration so important?

A Not many people know this, but about a third of the oxygen we breathe comes from ocean life. So the ocean is very important for us and our planet. Yet we know so little about it and how it works, especially the deep ocean. As we explore, we learn how we can help protect our oceans for the future.

giant ....
tube
worms

Today's explorers

These people never stop exploring. They take dangerous journeys and push themselves to the limit to find out more about our world – and way beyond.

Erik Weihenmayer

OCCUPATION:
Adventurer
CLAIM TO FAME:
Weihenmayer is the only blind person to have climbed Mount Everest.

Sylvia Earle

OCCUPATION:
Ocean explorer
CLAIM TO FAME:
Earle has spent over 7,000 hours studying underwater and has even lived in an undersea laboratory!

Laura Dekker

OCCUPATION:
Sailor
CLAIM TO FAME:
In 2012, at the age of 16, Dekker became the youngest person to complete a solo sail around the world.

Conrad Hoskin

OCCUPATION:
Rainforest explorer
CLAIM TO FAME:
In 2013, Hoskin was one of the first to explore the Cape Melville rainforest in Australia.

All these people prove that

In total, Williams has spent over 50 hours on space walks (out in the open in space, not inside a vehicle).

Hillary didn't start training to go to the poles until her 60s, when she had retired!

SOUTH POLE ➤

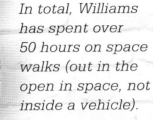

Sunita Williams

OCCUPATION:
Astronaut
CLAIM TO FAME:
Williams holds the record for the longest single spaceflight by a woman.

Robbie Shone

OCCUPATION:
Cave explorer/ photographer
CLAIM TO FAME:
Shone has discovered and photographed many record-breaking caves.

Ed Stafford

OCCUPATION:
Amazon walker
CLAIM TO FAME:
Stafford was the first person to walk the length of the River Amazon.

Barbara Hillary

OCCUPATION:
Polar explorer
CLAIM TO FAME:
At the age of 79, Hillary became the first African American woman to ski to both poles!

whoever you are, you can do it, too!

Glossary

accelerate
To get faster and faster.

amputate
To cut off a body part, usually because it is damaged.

asteroid
A small rocky object that travels around the Sun.

astronaut
A person who travels into space.

avalanche
A large amount of snow and ice that suddenly slides or falls down the side of a mountain.

bandit
A violent robber, usually one who is in a gang.

bioluminescence
The light produced by living things such as fireflies and some sea creatures.

bubonic plague
A deadly disease transmitted to humans by infected fleas that live on rats. It causes swollen lumps on the body.

cannibal
A person who eats other humans.

chronometer
A very accurate clock, used to determine a ship's position at sea.

colony
A group of people who leave their country to settle in a new area. Their new settlement is controlled by their original country.

compass
A tool used for finding direction. It has a magnetized needle that turns so that it always points north.

conquistador
One of the Spanish explorers who conquered Mexico and Peru in the 1500s.

culture
The ideas, traditions, beliefs, and way of life of a group of people.

DNA
The molecule that carries inherited information in all living things. *DNA* stands for *deoxyribonucleic acid*.

empire
A group of countries that are all controlled by the same powerful ruler.

frostbite
Damage to a body part that occurs after it has been exposed to very cold temperatures.

illegal
Against the law.

junk
A boat with square sails and a flat bottom, originally from China.

longship

A long, narrow ship with oars and one square sail, used by the Vikings.

malaria

A serious disease transmitted to humans by a particular kind of mosquito. It causes fever, chills, and sweating.

mutiny

A rebellion against or refusal to obey authority, especially in the military.

navigate

To plan a vehicle's path and steer it along that path.

pilgrimage

A journey to a holy place. The hajj is a pilgrimage that Muslims make to Mecca.

plunder

To steal goods or valuables by force.

satellite

A spacecraft that travels around Earth and collects scientific information or transmits messages.

scurvy

A disease caused by a lack of vitamin C. It causes damage to teeth and bones.

sextant

A tool used to determine a ship's position at sea. It measures the angle between the horizon and the Sun, the Moon, or a particular star.

slave

A person who is owned by another person and thought of as property.

submersible

A vehicle that can travel underwater.

typhoid

A serious disease caused by germs in food or water. It causes fever and diarrhoea.

Viking

A member of one of the northern peoples who invaded the coasts of Europe and explored the North American coast over 1,000 years ago.

Index

Thank you

Alamy Images: 28 bl (avadaRM), 48 l (Buddy Mays), 23 tl (Chris Hellier), 23 tr (Chris Willson), 19 tl, 30 t (Classic Image), 48 portraits (Everett Collection Historical), 6, 7 (Geoff Renner/Robert Harding World Imagery), 61 cbr (H.R. Bowers/Royal Geographical), 12 tr, 13 tl (Heritage Image Partnership Ltd), 52 c portrait (Historical image collection by Bildagentur-online), 36 tl portrait (Interfoto), 19 tc, 24 r (Ivy Close Images), 8 tl (Juan Antonio Guerrero Escobar), 23 cr, 38 b (Kasia Nowak), 64 bl portrait (Maciej Wojtkowiak), 67 ct (Marc Muench), 16 br, 17 bl (Mary Evans Picture Library), 9 r (NASA Archive), 18 bc, 41 cr, 49 tl (North Wind Picture Archives), 52 b portrait (nsf), 9 bc (Pete Mcbride/National Geographic Image Collection), 10 r (Peter Matthews), 8 br, 54 r, 60 t portrait (Pictorial Press Ltd), 22 br (Prisma Archivo), 61 t (PV Collection), 75 bcl (Robbie Shone), 46 tl (Simon Grosset), 16 cbr (The Art Gallery Collection), 72 b (WENN Ltd); AP Images: 59 cl (Bettmann/Corbis), 74 bl (DB Michael Brown/picture-alliance/dpa), 11 cbl (Evert-Jan Daniels), 11 cbr, 61 bl (Geoff Caddick), 74 bcr (Judy Fitzpatrick), 71 tl (RMS *Titanic*, Inc.), 11 bl (US Navy), 9 br; Barbara Hillary/www.barbarahillary.com: 75 br; Bridgeman Art Library: 34 bl inset (Columbus says goodbye to chief Guacanagarix in Hispaniola, Spanish School, (19th century)/Private Collection/Look and Learn), 50 fg (Lewis and Clark with Sacagawea (color litho) (detail), Paxson, Edgar Samuel (1852–1915)/Private Collection/Peter Newark American Pictures); Corbis Images/STF/epa: 27 tr inset; Courtesy, Conrad Hoskin: 74 br; Dr. Cindy Lee Van Dover: 72 tr; Dreamstime: 48 t (Aleksandra Gigowska), cover cb bg (Andreykuzmin), cover c fg b bg (Eti Swinford), cover ct bg (Maksim Shmeljov), cover c bg, back cover c bg (Paologozzi), cover c fg t bg (Sergii Kolesnyk), cover br (Yuriy Chaban); Ed Stafford: 75 bcr; Eric Tepe: 45 r; Fotolia: 25 cbc (Africa Studio), 31 tc (Amy_fang), 28 signpost (Andrey Kuzmin), 59 t frame (DAN), 29 t (Dmitry Pichugin), 53 lion (Eric Isselée), 13 crb (Fotofermer), 37 br gold (indigolotos), 22 l (quasarphotos), 52 cb bg, 53 cb bg (Ruth Hallam), 25 cbl (Soni Images Work), 28 caterpillar (sweetcrisis), 24 bg paper, 25 bg paper (Taddeus), 45 c, 55 r bg (Tryfonov), 25 t, 28 grass (Unclesam), 28 br rat (wildcat78), 58 br (ykumsri); Fundacion Nao Victoria: 11 ctl, 40 tr; Getty Images: 5 b, 36 br statue, 37 bl statue (Carl Court/Stringer/AFP), 27 helmet (Danita Delimont), 19 tr, 29 bc, 36 tc portrait (De Agostini), 17 tl (De Agostini Picture Library), 26 t (French School/The Bridgeman Art Library), 68 bc (Gamma-Keystone), 73 sub (Henry Groskinsky/The LIFE Images Collection), 47 cr (Johann Zoffany/The Bridgeman Art Library), 65 tr (Jun Sato/WireImage), 71 tr (Keipher McKennie), 14 bc, 44 l (Leemage/Universal Images Group), 31 tl (Persian School/The Bridgeman Art Library), 61 ctl, 61 br, 61 ctr, 62, 63 (Popperfoto), cover c fg (Robert F. Sisson/National Geographic), 20, 21 (Theodore de Bry/The Bridgeman Art Library), 27 sword (Viking/The Bridgeman Art Library), 12 l (Walter Meayers Edwards/National Geographic), 71 bc (William Frederick Mitchell/De Agostini Picture Library); iStockphoto: 47 t, 62 ice, 63 ice (07_av), 70 whale icon (Ace_Create), 68 bl (Alex Kotlov), 60 gramophone (AlexAvich), 33 tc turquoise (alexhstock), 37 cr (AlonzoDesign), 32 tl frame, 36 tl frame, 48 r frame, 52 t frame, 52 b frame, 60 t frame (Andrea Preibisch), 60 horse icon (AndreAnita), 74 snow, 75 snow (Andreas Herpens), 43 tl (AngiePhotos), 52 c insect, 53 side view insects, 53 top view insect (Antagain), 41 br bike icon (appleuzr), 28 t rat (Argument), 74 mask (belterz), 61 ctc (Björn Meyer), 44 bg, 45 bg, 54 bg, 55 bg (blackred), 53 hippo (Bobbushphoto), 70 c bg, 72 t bg, 73 t bg (BobHemphill), 64 tl (Brilt), 41 br boat icon, 60 people icon, 68 people icon (browndogstudios), 13 tr (bxzhit), 37 c (carlosphotos), 8 bl (Catherine Lane), 68 bg, 69 bg (clearviewstock), 58 r snow (coloroftime), 10 tr, 75 headlamp (cris180), 36 tc frame, 40 tl frame, 48 l frame, 52 c frame, 60 b frame (csheezio), 2 b, 75 butterfly (Dean_Fikar), 41 c cookie (dearbear), 29 br (Deejpilot), 24 tl (DennyThurstonPhotography), 35 crb, 37 crb (doodlemachine), 59 cr (duncan1890), 18 br, 32 tl portrait (ecliff6), 41 c biscuit (Eerik), 44 br (Ekely), 47 c (ekvals), 37 br (Electric_Crayon), 41 c maggots (empire331), 23 cl, 23 bl (enter89), 25 cbr (galdzer), 4 t, 5 t, 28 t bg, 29 t bg, 78, 79 (Gannet77), 16 t (GeorgiosArt), 60 husky icon (GlobalP), 65 hand icon (GlobalStock), 19 bl, 33 tr portrait, 40 tl portrait (Grafissimo), 32 bg water, 33 bg water, 70 l bg (gremlin), 13 br (HadelProductions), 59 photo corners (hanibaram), 27 baby icon (heather_mcgrath), 69 br (Heidi Kristensen), 32 b gold, 33 b gold, 33 b gold (hidesy), 36 bl gold (idal), 11 tl (IlexImage), 22 bg, 23 bg (imagedepotpro), 22 bc waves, 23 bg waves (irabell), 52 snake (irin717), 27 snowflake icon (Irochka_T), 43 cl (isgaby), 69 cr (iStackphotons), 41 tr (Ivan Bliznetsov), 37 crt (IvanGuevara), 25 cb bg (ixsblue), 74 hat (Jack_Art), 10 ctr (jamesbenet), 30 border, 31 border (javarman3), 31 tr (javi_martin), 52 t globes, 52 b globe, 74 globe (jimmyjamesbond), 13 cl (JLGutierrez), 58 bg, 59 bg (jmbatt), 70 bl (joebrandt), 2 bg, 3 bg, 64 bg, 65 bg (johnason), 14 cursor (Just_Human), 49 cr (Justin Horrocks), 35 br (Kathy Konkle), 10 tc (Kerstin Waurick), 75 frog (kikkerdirk), 8 bg, 9 bg (komisar), 32 fg map, 33 fg map (konradlew), 10 cbl fg (KrivoTIFF), 9 bl (kurapy11), 32 ct flag (Lingbeek), 25 b (lnzyx), 49 lamp (luna4), 28 headstone (ManuelVelasco), 60 compass (Mark7GD), 35 tr (MarkM73), 58 l snow, 59 snow (mercedes rancaño), 52 b bg, 53 b bg (MichaelDeckert), 64 tr (mikeuk), 33 tl spices (MKucova), 47 cl (Mienny), 28 cl (Moncherie), 52 t bg, 53 t bg (mountainberryphoto),

70 br frame, 71 frames (Mustilk), 55 l (Nancy Nehring), 74 bg, 75 bg (Nastco), 53 old paper (Nic_Taylor), 55 r fg (nicoolay), 17 br (Oktay Ortakcioglu), 69 bl (orestegaspari), 31 br (oversnap), 32 cb flag (PaulCowan), 49 r elk (PaulTessier), 27 crown icon, 35 crt (PhotoHamster), 35 cross (Piter1977), 10 ctl, 48 b, 64 bl (powerofforever), 18 tl, 19 br (raclro), 31 cb (rhyman007), 24 bl (Rivendellstudios), 24 bg map, 25 bg map, 44 border, 45 border, 54 border, 55 border, 58 border, 59 border (Roberto A Sanchez), 9 cr (rodho), 49 l elk (rpbirdman), 60 huskies (Saksoni), 41 cl (Saracin), 68 t (scibak), 37 tr (seamartini), 54 l (seaskylab), 10 b bg, 11 b bg (shaunl), back cover b (skodonnell), 49 b (Skyhobo), 17 tc (StephanHoerold), 52 ct bg, 53 ct bg (stevenallan), 46 b, 47 bl (Studio-Annika), 2 t, 75 astronaut (suriyasilsaksom), 15 t (threeart), 74 sailboat (travenian), 31 c (tropicalpixsingapore), 33 tl bird (tunart), 12 bg, 13 bg (urosr), 10 tl, 75 boots (Vasiliki Varvaki), 27 cross icon (vectorkingdom), 32 l icons, 33 r icons (Vertyr), 65 c (vidalidali), 38 t (vikif), 22 tr (Volant.nevist), 4 tr, 28 bl rat, 43 tc (wildcat78), 74 skis (wingmar), 52 t portrait (wynnter), 13 crt (Zocha_K); Library of Congress/Illus. in: *Mammoth Cave*, by Hovey, 1882, p. 7.: 16 ct; Courtesy of Mary Levy Goldiner: 17 tr; Missouri History Museum, St. Louis: 59 br; NASA: 11 ctcr (Bill Ingalls), 11 ctr (Boeing), 14 bg, 15 bg (Jesse Allen), back cover t bg, cover t bg, cover tl, 11 tr, 11 ctcl, 17 cr, 69 tl, 69 tr; National Geographic Stock: 64 fg, 65 fg (Alfred Gregory, Royal Geographic Society), cover bl (Natalie B. Fobes), 67 cb (Stephen Alvarez); Newscom/CB2/ZOB/WENN.com: 15 b; NOAA: 71 br (Archival Photography by Steve Nicklas, NOS, NGS), 73 b (Okeanos Explorer Program, Galapagos Rift Expedition 2011), 1, 56, 57 (T. Kerby/OAR/National Undersea Research Program (NURP); Univ. of Hawaii), 70 tl; Robbie Shone: 66, 67 l bg, 67 b; Science Source: 10 bl (Adam Jones), 43 br (Biophoto Associates), 74 bcl (Connie Bransilver), 71 bl (Dr. Ken MacDonald), 35 c (Mary Evans), 47 br (Meredith Carlson), 41 cl bg (oleandra), 43 cr (Oleksii Iezhov), 50 bg, 51 fire (Petrenko Andriy), 32 whale icon, 32 shrimp icon, 32 starfish icon, 33 shrimp icon, 33 (pio3), 75 tree (polaris50d), 70 80 (sergign), 74 tree (Taras Tischenko Irina), 16 bg, 17 bg 49 tr (Valentyna Chukhlyebova), (vitmark), 75 tree trunk (Vlue), 38 Thinkstock/RTimages: 12 br, 13 bl; Illustration: 11 bc, 16 cl, 26 b, 27 bg, 42, Powell Survey: 53 bc.

Shutterstock, Inc.: 10 cbl bg (Andrea Izzotti), 40 bg, 41 bg (Anton Balazh), 49 kettle (apiguide), 18 bg, 19 bg, 25 ct, 29 c, 40 bl (AridOcean), 60 bg, 61 bg (axily), 75 b plant (Cantonatty), 48 c bg, 49 c bg (Christopher Boswell), 12 tr bg, 13 tl bg, 32 bg paper, 33 bg paper (Cranach), 27 ax (Creative HQ), 67 t (Diana Nikolaeva Dimitrova), 18 bl, 27 cr icon, 30 bl icon, 46 l icon (Epsicons), 28 tl (grintan), 33 whale icon (Hein Nouwens), 32 ship icon (Henner Damke), 16 all frames (Iakov Filimonov), 17 all frames, 45 l (jbmake), 40 bc (Jeffrey B. Banke), 30 bg, 31 bg (La India Piaroa), 74 parrot (Lakeview Images), cover b bg, back cover b bg (Lawrence Cruciana), 41 bl inset (Lena Lir), 75 signpost (LilKar), 35 cr (lisboaimagelab), 74 rain (Magnia), 27 passport, 28 passport, 34 passport, 41 passport, 61 passport, 64 passport (Mark Carrel), back cover t (Monkey Business Images), 60 labels (My Life Graphic), 31 ct fg, 31 b fg (oleandra), (Peter Kunasz), 49 icons, 32 octopus icon, 33 pufferfish octopus icon br (Rich Carey), Vyshnya, 76, 77 (toadberry), 40 br, 36 bg, 37 bg bg, 39 (worradirek); Tim Loughhead/Precision 43 bg, 70 sub art; USGS/

(nelik), 3 b, 75 shuttle (Nerthuz), 30 b